Emergency Rescue

by Camilla Gersh

Series Editor Deborah Lock
Project Editor Caryn Jenner
Editor Nandini Gupta
Designer Charlotte Jennings
Art Editor Yamini Panwar
Senior Art Editor Ann Cannings

Producer, Pre-production Nadine King
DTP Designers Nand Kishor Acharya, Dheeraj Singh
Picture Researcher Nishwan Rasool
Managing Editor Soma B. Chowdhury
Managing Art Editor Ahlawat Gunjan
Art Director Martin Wilson

Reading Consultant
Jacqueline Harris

Subject Consultants
Keith Green, Firefighter
Paul Adams, Paramedic

First published in Great Britain in 2016
by Dorling Kindersley Limited
80 Strand, London, WC2R 0RL

A CIP catalogue record for this book
is available from the British Library
ISBN: 978-0-2412-2508-0

Printed and bound in China.
The publisher would like to thank the following for their kind permission to reproduce their photographs:
(Key: a=above, b=below/bottom, c=centre, l=left, r=right, t=top)

1 Dreamstime.com: Victoria Whitehead. 2 iStockphoto.com: AlexSava (br); franckreporter (bc). 2–3 Dreamstime.com: Mike_kiev (b). 3 Alamy Images: J Orr (tr). Getty Images: Valerie Macon (br). 4 Alamy Images: Hirdes/F1online digitale Bildagentur GmbH (t). Getty Images: Valerie Macon (bc). 4–5 Dreamstime.com: Mike_kiev (b). 5 Alamy Images: Eric Nathan (b). 6 iStockphoto.com: webphotographeer (t). 6–7 Dreamstime.com: Mike_kiev (b). 7 Corbis: Mike Kemp/Rubberball. 8 iStockphoto.com: webphotographeer (t). 8–9 Dreamstime.com: Mike_kiev (b). 9 iStockphoto.com: AlexSava (bl); webphotographeer (b). 10 Dreamstime.com: Mamuka Gotsiridze (bl). 11 Dreamstime.com: Mamuka Gotsiridze (br). 12 Alamy Images: Hirdes/F1online digitale Bildagentur GmbH (t). Getty Images: Valerie Macon (bl). 12–13 Dreamstime.com: Durvidanoar; Mike_kiev (b). 14 Getty Images: Valerie Macon (br); Oli Scarff (t). 14–15 Dreamstime.com: Mike_kiev (b). 15 Dreamstime.com: Sandra Van Der Steen (c). 16 iStockphoto.com: anthonysp (t). 16–17 Dreamstime.com: Mike_kiev (b). 17 Getty Images: Valerie Macon (bl). iStockphoto.com: andipantz (c). 18–19 Corbis: Keith Dannemiller (t). Dreamstime.com: Mike_kiev (b). 19 Getty Images: Valerie Macon (bc). 20 Alamy Images: Tony Kwan (crb); Sunpix (c). Dreamstime.com: Mamuka Gotsiridze (bl). Getty Images: Jewel Samad/AFP Photo (clb). 21 Alamy Images: Martyn Goddard (cl); Markus Keller/imageBROKER (cr); Nik Taylor (clb). Dreamstime.com: Mamuka Gotsiridze (b). 22 Dreamstime.com: Mamuka Gotsiridze (bl); Santiphoto (c). 22–23 Dreamstime.com: Qtrix. 23 Dreamstime.com: Mamuka Gotsiridze (br). 24 Dreamstime.com: Mamuka Gotsiridze (br). 25 Dreamstime.com: Mamuka Gotsiridze (br). 26 Alamy Images: Hirdes/F1online digitale Bildagentur GmbH (t). 26–27 Dreamstime.com: Mike_kiev (b). 27 PunchStock: Blend Images. 28–29 123RF.com: federicofoto (t). 28 Dreamstime.com: Mike_kiev (b). 30 Dreamstime.com: Mamuka Gotsiridze (bl); Nejron (c). 31 Dreamstime.com: Mamuka Gotsiridze (b); Nejron (c). 32–33 Dreamstime.com: Mike_kiev (b). 33 Dorling Kindersley: Bergen County, NJ, Law and Public Safety Institute (t). 34 Corbis: Chris Carroll. 34–35 Dreamstime.com: Mike_kiev (b). 36 Dreamstime.com: Mamuka Gotsiridze (bl). Getty Images: Bloomberg (crb). iStockphoto.com: hartphotography1 (cra). 37 Alamy Images: Victor Nikitin (crb). Dreamstime.com: Mamuka Gotsiridze (br). Getty Images: Glenn Asakawa (cra). 38 Alamy Images: Hirdes/F1online digitale Bildagentur GmbH (t). iStockphoto.com: AlexSava (bc). 38–39 Dreamstime.com: Mike_kiev (b). 39 Corbis: Zero Creatives (t). 40–41 Dreamstime.com: Mike_kiev (b). 40 iStockphoto.com: AlexSava (b). 41 Dorling Kindersley: London Ambulance Service (c). 42 Alamy Images: one-image photography (b). 42–43 Dreamstime.com: Mike_kiev (b). 43 iStockphoto.com: franckreporter (br). 44–45 123RF.com: Pat Olson (t). Dreamstime.com: Mike_kiev (b). 45 iStockphoto.com: AlexSava (bc). 46 Alamy Images: Hirdes/F1online digitale Bildagentur GmbH (t). iStockphoto.com: franckreporter (bc). 46–47 Dreamstime.com: Mike_kiev (b). 47 iStockphoto.com: gsmudger (t). 48 Alamy Images: FEMA (t). iStockphoto.com: franckreporter (br). 48–49 Dreamstime.com: Mike_kiev (b). 50 Corbis: KIM KYUNG-HOON/Reuters (t). 50–51 Dreamstime.com: Mike_kiev (b). 51 iStockphoto.com: franckreporter (t). 52–53 Dreamstime.com: Mike_kiev (b). 52 iStockphoto.com: AlexSava (br); franckreporter (bc). 53 Alamy Images: Tom Grill/Corbis (c). Getty Images: Valerie Macon (br). 54 Dreamstime.com: Mamuka Gotsiridze (bl). iStockphoto.com: Yuri_Arcurs (cra); Figure8Photos (clb). 55 Alamy Images: Picture Partners (tr). Dreamstime.com: Mamuka Gotsiridze (br). 56–57 iStockphoto.com: t3000 (All Footprints). 57 Dreamstime.com: Mamuka Gotsiridze (bl). 58 Dreamstime.com: Mamuka Gotsiridze (br). 58 Getty Images: Valerie Macon (bc). 58–59 Dreamstime.com: Mike_kiev (b). 59 iStockphoto.com: AlexSava (bl); franckreporter (br). 60–61 Dreamstime.com: Mike_kiev (b). 60 Dreamstime.com: David Fowler (tr). Getty Images: Valerie Macon (bc). 61 iStockphoto.com: AlexSava (bl); franckreporter (br)

Jacket images: Front: Corbis: Darren Greenwood; Dorling Kindersley: Bergen County, NJ, Law and Public Safety Institute br, B&O Railroad Museum cr; Back: Dreamstime.com: Fg76 l; iStockphoto.com: gsmudger r; Spine: PunchStock: Blend Images
All other images © Dorling Kindersley
For further information see: www.dkimages.com

A WORLD OF IDEAS:
SEE ALL THERE IS TO KNOW

www.dk.com

Contents

What's Your Emergency?

It's an **emergency**! Someone is in danger and needs urgent help. What should you do?

Call 9-9-9. This is the telephone number for the emergency services. Your call will be answered by an emergency **controller**, whose job it is to tell police, fire or medical services about emergencies.

A controller will ask you what the emergency is and where it is happening. Emergency controllers need to be able to think quickly and stay calm. They are trained to handle lots of different situations and will help you with all kinds of emergencies.

If you call 9-9-9, you will be put through to an emergency call centre. Sometimes, a computer can detect your **location**, but the controller will always check your address anyway.

The controller will take details of your emergency and contact your nearest police, fire department or ambulance service. All of this happens in just a few minutes.

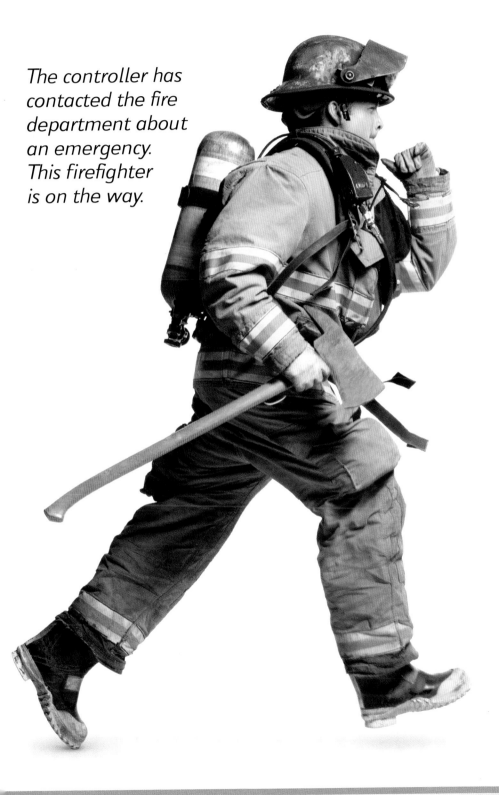

The controller has contacted the fire department about an emergency. This firefighter is on the way.

Emergency controllers often stay on the phone until help arrives. They talk to callers to keep them calm. Most importantly, they tell the caller what to do until the emergency services arrive.

They can even tell callers how to give first aid if someone is choking or having a heart attack. Emergency controllers save many lives.

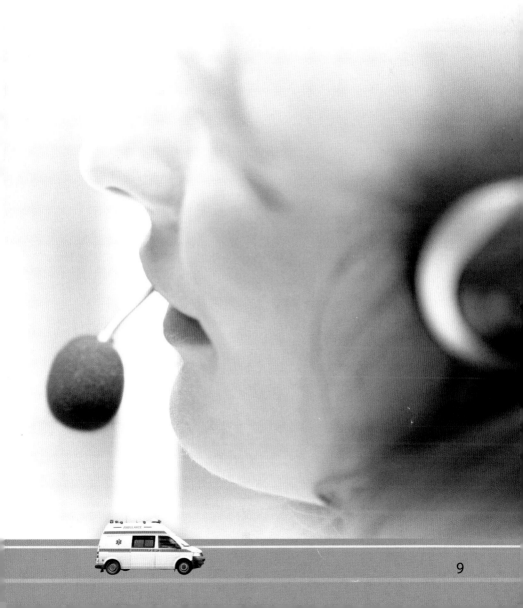

What to Do in an Emergency

Call **9-9-9** if there may be danger or someone is hurt.

Call 9-9-9

- Say your name and where you are.

- Explain why you need help.

- Follow the controller's instructions.

Remember:
try to stay calm.

If there's a fire

- Leave the building as quickly as you can.
- Crawl on the floor if there is smoke.
- Don't go back into the building.

If you need the police

- Go to a safe place right away.

If you need a doctor

- Don't move the person who is sick or hurt.

Be prepared for an **emergency**

- Memorise your parents' or carers' phone numbers.
- Post emergency numbers near the phone.
- Talk with your parents or carers about what to do in different emergency situations.
- With your family, pick a safe place to go in case of emergencies, such as the house of a neighbour you trust.

Chapter 1
POLICE

> *Help! Somebody broke into our house. Please come!*

The police usually handle emergencies that involve crime. A crime is when someone breaks the law.

For example, a person breaking into someone else's house is a crime. People can help police stop crimes by reporting **suspicious** activity. This might include seeing a stranger go into a neighbour's house when no one's home or hearing someone scream. You should report suspicious activity by calling 9-9-9.

Police officers in the United Kingdom

The loud noise of a **siren** means the police are on their way to an emergency. The siren tells other drivers to get out of the way!

Police often wear **uniforms** so people know who they are. Sometimes they wear protective clothing as part of their uniform.

Police need special equipment to do their job. Most officers carry a weapon to defend themselves and a radio to speak to other police. They use handcuffs so suspected criminals can't get away.

The police handcuff a suspect to take to the police station.

Clues, such as fingerprints or traces of saliva, help **detectives** *solve a crime.*

Police do different jobs. For example, detectives **investigate** complicated crimes. Traffic police keep order on the roads. Specially trained police help in situations such as rescuing **hostages**.

Many police officers **patrol** neighbourhoods to keep them safe. Some police drive patrol cars, while others ride on bicycles or horses, or even in boats or helicopters.

Police in Philadelphia, Pennsylvania, USA

What does a police detective do?

If you want to be a police officer, you need to be physically fit and have lots of common sense. Police officers train at a police headquarters. There, they learn about the law, first aid and how to use police equipment.

Police training in Mexico

They also need to do field training. This means teaming up with an experienced officer to get practise on the job. That way, they'll know what to do in different situations once they become police officers.

In Pursuit

Police use different ways of getting around, depending on where they are. It also depends whether they are on patrol or on their way to an emergency!

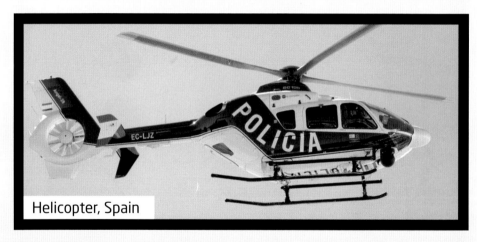

Helicopter, Spain

Jetski, Australia

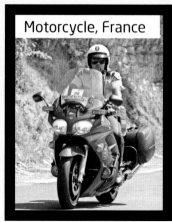

Motorcycle, France

Boat, Slovenia

Horse, Canada

Snowmobile, Germany

Bicycle, UK

Patrol car, USA

Police Radio Codes

In some places, emergency controllers speak to the police on radios using special codes. These are the codes in the USA.

"51, a 211 at 2020 Sunset!"

This means: "Calling police officer with badge number 51. There's a robbery at the address 2020 Sunset Street."

Here are some radio codes used by controllers and police officers in the USA:

Use these radio codes to work out what this means:

"A 925 in a 503. Code 2."

10-4	Ok
211	Robbery
503	Stolen vehicle
901	Traffic accident
901-N	Ambulance needed
904	Fire
925	Suspicious person
999	Officer needs help. EMERGENCY!

Code 1	Normal. Take this call next.
Code 2	Urgent! Hurry, but follow traffic laws. No red light or siren.
Code 3	Emergency! Use red light and siren.
Code 4	No further assistance needed.

Answer: A suspicious person in a stolen vehicle. Urgent! Hurry, but follow traffic laws. No red light or siren.

Fingerprints

Sometimes, criminals leave fingerprints behind. Everyone's fingerprints are unique, so they can be a useful clue in identifying a criminal.

A fingerprint kit might contain:

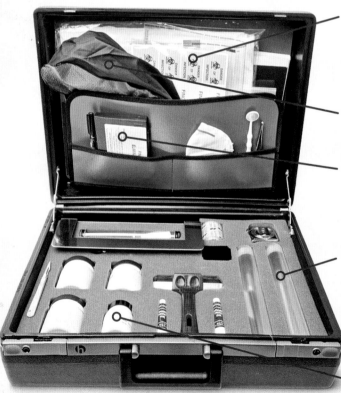

Evidence labels

Shoe covers

Fingerprint ink pad

Magnetic fingerprint brushes

Dusting powder

Step 1

Crime scene scientists use fine powder and a soft brush to gently dust the surface where fingerprints might be.

Step 2

They press clear tape on to the dusted print, and then peel it off so that the print comes with it.

Step 3

Fingerprints found at a crime scene are identified using a computerised system.

Chapter 2
FIRE

Help! My house is on fire!

Firefighters put out fires, rescue people from fires, and provide first aid to people involved in a fire. When they receive an emergency call, they zoom off in the fire engine as quickly as they can!

Firefighters work either a shift during the day or during the night. They spend most of their time doing jobs around the fire station, exercising, training and practising a variety of **drills** for emergencies.

Sometimes they teach other people how to prevent fires. They might even come to your school!

A firefighter slides quickly down the fire pole on his way to an emergency.

Firefighters need to bring a lot of equipment on their engines. This includes first aid supplies, ladders, **fire extinguishers** and tools for breaking down doors or cutting cars open.

Fire engines also carry about 300 m (1,000 feet) of hose and hose reels. Firefighters pump water from the fire engine through the hose. Then they spray the water on the fire to put it out.

FIRE GEAR

Firefighters often have to get very close to fires, so their clothing and equipment protects them.

Helmet with visor protects head and eyes.

Hood protects neck.

Mask prevents breathing in smoke.

Tunic, leggings and gloves resist heat and fire.

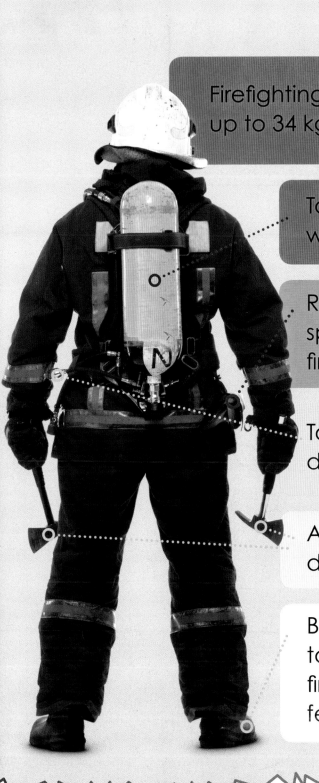

Firefighting gear weighs up to 34 kg (75 lbs).

Tank is filled with fresh air.

Radio used to speak to other firefighters.

Torch used for dark places.

Axes break down doors.

Boots with steel toes protect firefighters' feet.

Three things are needed for a fire: air, heat and fuel. These are called the 'triangle of fire'. Paper, wood, and petrol are some examples of fuel. To put out a fire, firefighters usually try to get rid of the air and heat by covering the fire with lots of water.

In a forest fire, firefighters often try
to remove the fuel, too. This is to make
a 'fire break'. Trees are the fuel in a
forest fire. If firefighters destroy the trees
in the fire's path, there will be no more
trees for the fire to burn. That way, they
can save the rest of the forest.

This firefighter uses a special saw to free passengers trapped in a car accident.

Firefighters need to be strong and physically fit. They also have to be brave and able to stay calm under pressure.

Firefighters do lots of training. They learn about fire and how it can spread. They learn how to use firefighting and first aid equipment. They also learn about dangerous chemicals so they can make places safe after a chemical leak or spill. Firefighters practise rescuing people from car accidents, too.

Why do firefighters have to learn about dangerous chemicals?

Firefighter's Routine

Firefighters work in shifts. There must be firefighters on duty day and night. They always need to be ready in case of an emergency!

9:30–11:00 AM

Day shift begins. Check fire engines are working and stocked with supplies. Complete other jobs around the station.

11:30 AM–1.00 PM

Drills and training. This might be on firefighting techniques, first aid, or preventing fires.

1:00–2.00 PM

Lunch break.

2:00–8:00 PM

Home fire safety visits (HFSV) to help people in their homes to be fire safe. Also school and club visits. Final checks and complete reports.

8:00 PM

Night shift arrives and takes over. Check equipment and fire engines are stocked with supplies. Attend training talks. Complete reports.

After midnight

Bedtime.

9:30 AM

The day shift reports for duty. The night shift returns home.

Chapter 3
AMBULANCE

> *Help! My husband's having a heart attack!*

Paramedics give people emergency medical care. They are trained in first aid and other kinds of medical treatment. Paramedics often drive to emergencies in ambulances, which have sirens just like police cars or fire engines.

Paramedics help if someone has a serious illness, a heart attack, or been hurt in an accident. They provide quick lifesaving treatment and take injured or sick people to hospital to be treated by doctors. Sometimes paramedics deliver babies when people can't get to a hospital.

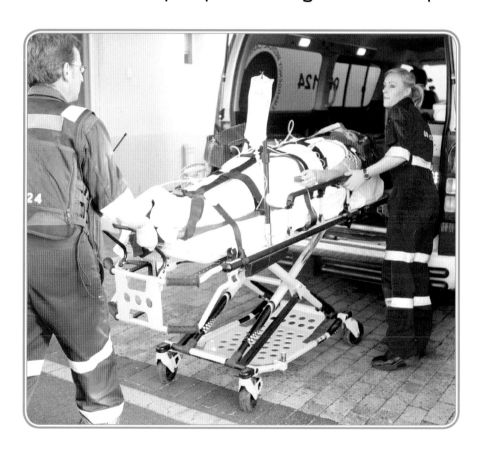

Paramedics take lots of important equipment in the ambulance. Along with bandages and other basic first aid supplies, they have special stretcher beds and chairs for very sick patients that can be taken out of the ambulance.

They take oxygen tanks and different masks to help people breathe. They also have a special machine that can measure people's heart rates, blood pressure and oxygen levels. This machine is also a defibrillator, which uses electricity to shock someone's heart to help it beat normally again if it stops.

When paramedics treat people, they wear protective gloves. This prevents passing **germs** to the patients and also protects paramedics from infections.

Sterile dressings   Emergency medications   Bandages

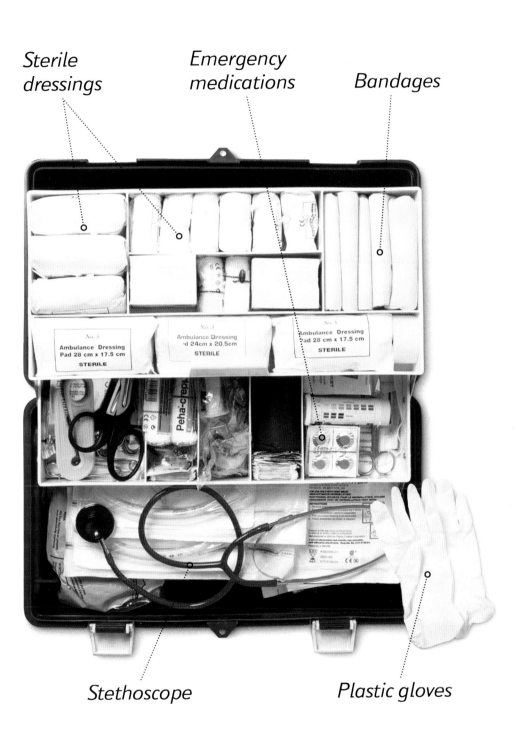

Stethoscope   Plastic gloves

There are different levels of paramedics, depending on how much training they have had. Consultant paramedics are the most trained. Paramedics are allowed to give certain medicines to patients as part of their

care to make them better, to stop pain, or to save their lives. Some police officers are also trained as paramedics.

Paramedics don't just travel in ambulances. Some paramedics travel in cars or helicopters, or on motorcycles or bicycles.

What is the most trained paramedic level called?

A paramedic on a motorcycle is often quicker and will give emergency care while waiting for an ambulance.

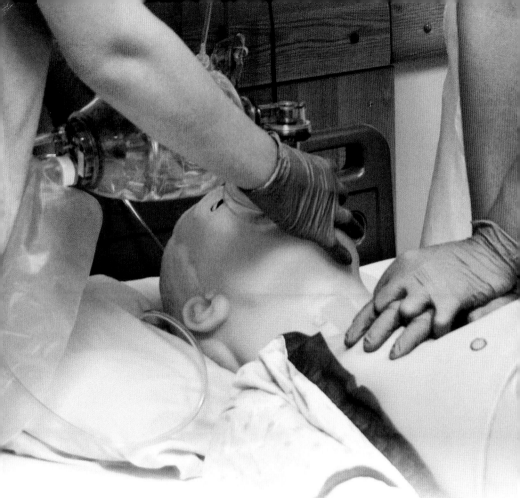

To be a paramedic, you must be able
to stay calm and make decisions quickly.
You also need to be physically fit and
strong enough to lift patients.

Paramedics have special training
to deal with many different medical
emergencies. They learn lifesaving

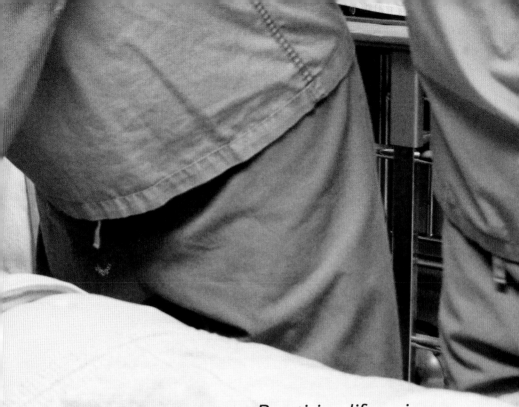

Practising lifesaving on a mannequin.

techniques to keep the blood and oxygen circulating around the body. They learn to monitor a patient's vital signs, including breathing and pulse. They also learn to put bandages on different types of wounds. Paramedics learn all about how the body works and how to help when people are ill.

45

Chapter 4

SPECIAL
SERVICES

Help! I'm stuck on a mountain and I can't get back down....

Sometimes other emergency services are needed, such as a search-and-rescue team. Their job is to find lost people and rescue them from dangerous situations.

A team member is lowered down to the rescue site.

Search-and-rescue teams find and rescue people from places that are hard to reach. These places include oceans, forests, mountains, deserts, caves or mines. They often use helicopters to search from above. Once the rescue team locates the person who needs help, they may use other vehicles and equipment for the rescue.

A search-and-rescue team helps during a flood.

Search-and-rescue teams are not normally needed every day, so some teams are made up of **volunteers**. This means they give up their time to help others even though they don't get paid.

People who like adventure, especially being outdoors, might want to join a search-and-rescue team. Like other emergency teams, they usually have special training. They learn how to use search-and-rescue equipment, plus first aid and survival skills.

Search-and-rescue teams are especially good at following tracks to find clues of people who are missing. Many are also good at other outdoor skills, such as sailing or climbing mountains.

Emergency relief workers in Japan make their way through heavy snow.

Emergency relief is a special service that brings food, water and other urgent supplies to people affected by big emergencies. Disasters such as earthquakes, hurricanes and blizzards are rare, but they can affect a lot of people across a wide area. Sometimes emergency relief teams drop supplies from planes or helicopters if they can't reach affected areas.

The Red Cross and Peace Corps provide this service around the world. They work with police, firefighters, paramedics and search-and-rescue teams to help people survive disasters and get back to normal lives as quickly as possible.

Working for the emergency services may sound exciting, but it can be really scary, too. It's also hard work!

You can help the emergency services by talking to parents and teachers about how to stay safe and avoid emergencies.

Remember: don't call the emergency services unless there is an actual emergency. It will waste their time when they could be saving lives. Maybe one day you'll be the one saving lives!

How can you help the emergency services?

Rescue Animals

Animals are also used in the emergency services.

Dogs

Dogs have an incredible sense of smell. They can be trained by the police to find **illegal** things like drugs and bombs. These dogs form part of a K-9 unit.

Dogs are also extremely important to search-and-rescue teams and fire crews. They're very good at finding people. They can follow a trail with their noses, using the smell from a person's clothing.

Horses

Horses are used by both police and search-and-rescue teams. They can go to places that cars cannot. Horses might even be trained to find people using their sense of smell.

Rats

Scientists hope that rats might also be trained to search for people in places that humans can't reach.

Cockroaches

In the future, search-and-rescue teams might even use cockroaches with mini-microphones attached to find people trapped in small spaces.

How to Follow Tracks

Here are some tips on how to find someone by following their tracks the way search-and-rescue teams do.

1 ### Find a track

Look at the ground to find a footprint. An area that is smoother or flatter than the ground around it might be a footprint.

2 ### Describe the track

Measure the length and width of the footprint with a ruler. Write down a description. Is the toe round or square? Does the sole have a pattern?

3 Find the next track
Once you've found one track, you should be able to find others.

4 Measure the stride
Measure the distance between tracks to find out if the person takes long or short steps (the stride).

5 Look for other signs
Sweet wrappers, broken twigs, water splashed on rocks and pieces of thread from clothing might also be clues. Look for anything out of place.

Emergency Quiz

Find the answers to these questions about what you have read. Answer correctly and help the ambulance get to the hospital.

Key:
➡ Correct! Go ahead.
⛔ Wrong. No entry.

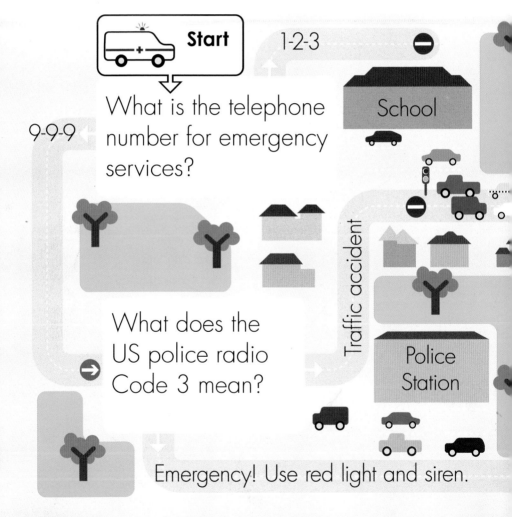

Start

1-2-3

School

9-9-9

What is the telephone number for emergency services?

Traffic accident

What does the US police radio Code 3 mean?

Police Station

Emergency! Use red light and siren.

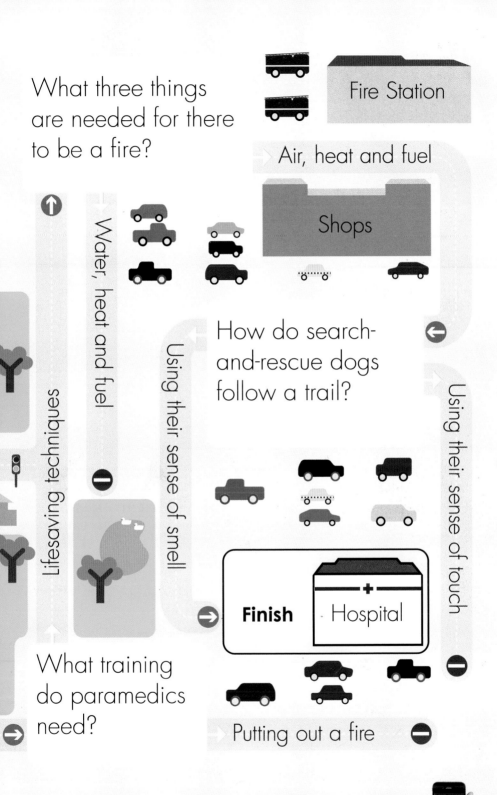

What three things
are needed for there
to be a fire?

Fire Station

Air, heat and fuel

Shops

Water, heat and fuel

Using their sense of smell

Lifesaving techniques

How do search-
and-rescue dogs
follow a trail?

Using their sense of touch

Finish Hospital

What training
do paramedics
need?

Putting out a fire

Glossary

controller
someone who sends people where they are needed

detective
police officer whose job is to investigate and solve crimes

drill
practice training

emergency
very serious and urgent situation

evidence
information gathered to prove that something is true

fire extinguisher
a container that releases a jet of water, foam, gas or other material to put out a fire

first aid
immediate help for injury or illness

germs
tiny living things that can get into your body and make you sick

hostages
people being held against their will

illegal
forbidden by law

investigate
explore or research
to find answers

location
particular position
or place

patrol
keeping watch
over an area

siren
alarm that makes
a long, loud sound
to warn people

suspicious
appearing to
be doing
something wrong

technique
way of doing
something

uniform
clothing worn by
members of the
same group or
organisation

volunteers
people who offer
their time to work
without being paid

Guide for Parents

DK Readers is a four-level interactive reading adventure series for children, developing the habit of reading widely for both pleasure and information. These chapter books have an exciting main narrative interspersed with a range of reading genres to suit your child's reading ability, as required by the National Curriculum. Each book is designed to develop your child's reading skills, fluency, grammar awareness, and comprehension in order to build confidence and engagement when reading.

Ready for a *Beginning to Read Alone* book

YOUR CHILD SHOULD

- be able to read most words without needing to stop and break them down into sound parts.
- read smoothly, in phrases and with expression.
  By this level, your child will be mostly reading silently.
- self-correct when some word or sentence doesn't sound right.

A VALUABLE AND SHARED READING EXPERIENCE

For some children, text reading, particularly non-fiction, requires much effort but adult participation can make this both fun and easier. So here are a few tips on how to use this book with your child.

TIP 1 **Check out the contents together before your child begins:**

- invite your child to check the blurb, contents page and layout of the book and comment on it.
- ask your child to make predictions about the narrative.
- chat about the information your child might want to find out.

TIP 2 **Encourage fluent and flexible reading:**

- support your child to read in fluent, expressive phrases, making full use of punctuation and thinking about the meaning.

- encourage your child to slow down and check information where appropriate.

TIP 3 Indicators that your child is reading for meaning:

- your child will be responding to the text if he/she is self-correcting and varying his/her voice.
- your child will want to talk about what he/she is reading or is eager to turn the page to find out what will happen next.

TIP 4 Praise, share and chat:

- encourage your child to recall specific details after each chapter.
- provide opportunities for your child to pick out interesting words and discuss what they mean.
- discuss how the author captures the reader's interest, or how effective the non-fiction layouts are.
- ask questions about the text. These help to develop comprehension skills and awareness of the language used.

A FEW ADDITIONAL TIPS

- Read to your child regularly to demonstrate fluency, phrasing and expression; to find out or check information; and for sharing enjoyment.
- Encourage your child to reread favourite texts to increase reading confidence and fluency.
- Check that your child is reading a range of different types, such as poems, jokes and following instructions.

Index